CRYSTAL CLEAR WATER

FASTEST, EASIEST AND CHEAPEST WAY TO A

BEAUTIFUL AQUARIUM

KEVIN MATOS

As simple and straight to the point as this book will be, it's only going to solve your cloudy water issues. But the Aquarium Hobby can be very overwhelming. I know, I've been there.

That's why I've created a 1 on 1 consultation service to provide immediate guidance with any issue you may have. Setting up a new tank? Trouble with tank cycling? Multiple fish death and no idea why? I can help.

Schedule your 1 on 1 phone call or zoom call and together we'll have your fish thriving, not just surviving!

Visit KaveManAquatics.com/KaveMan-Coaching for more info and scheduling.

To my wife who saw the passion inside me

and fueled my fire,

Thank you!

TABLE OF CONTENTS

Introduction

ITS ABOUT MORE THAN JUST CLEAR WATER

If you're reading this book, it's because you've found a joy in fish keeping. The hobby has ingulfed you and you're all in at this point. Your aquarium brings another form of beauty and fulfillment into your home. And if you haven't gotten attached to your fish yet, you will.

While this book is intended to help you make your aquarium display as beautiful as it can possibly be, and it will, I'd like you to keep in mind that our efforts shouldn't stop there.

We must keep in mind all the other responsibilities that come with keeping an aquarium and keeping our fish happy and healthy.

I say this because by the end of this book you will absolutely have crystal clear water in your tank, but that can be deceiving. Crystal clear *looking* water does not mean clean, healthy water.

Poisonous byproducts like ammonia, nitrite and nitrate are not visible to the naked eye.

While we do what we can to make our tanks beautiful and pleasing to our eyes, we must also ensure a clean, healthy environment for our wet pets!

The KaveMan Aquatics Website and YouTube channel has tons of helpful articles and videos to help you cover all the bases in the aquarium hobby. They're there if you need it!

KaveManAquatics.com

YouTube.com/KaveManAquatics

Part I

The Foundation Matters

KAVEMAN AQUATICS

Chapter 1

BACTERIAL BLOOM

> "You don't want to do excessive water changes or add a bunch of unnecessary products during this bacterial bloom."

Bacterial Bloom is usually the first type of cloudy water you'll encounter as a new fish keeper with a new, young tank setup. Which is why it's the first thing I want to cover in this book. The good news is it's perfectly normal. Bad news is there really isn't much you can do about it. Let me explain.

When your tank is new and freshly setup it hasn't grown the beneficial bacteria it needs to:

1.   Make your tank habitable for your fish and

2.   Help in keeping your tank water crystal clear.

Bacterial Bloom happens when Heterotrophic Bacteria grow in excess and populate your water column. They grow because of the dissolved organics in your source water. Without autotrophic bacteria present (aka

Beneficial Bacteria) they go wild and reproduce like jack rabbits. They're also bigger than your autotrophic bacteria and can be seen by the naked eye. This is what causes that cloudy, milky white look in your tank water.

Like I said though this is a normal occurrence in a new setup because your tank just hasn't had enough time to mature and grow the beneficial bacteria we want. But with time this cloudiness will subside on its own. It could take a few days, or a week +. You don't want to do excessive water changes or add a bunch of unnecessary products during this bacterial bloom. The key is just to be patient. I know though sometimes that's easier said than done. But stay strong and let your tank get through the cycle. Just trust me on this one 😊

Now if you think your tanks cloudiness is due to a bacterial bloom and it's NOT a new tank setup then you've got other problems. Something you are doing or something that has happened in your tank is causing the bloom and you've got to figure it out. Most of the tips coming up in this book will help in preventing something like this from happening. But if you're already there I highly suggest you check out my full article on bacterial blooms.

It can be found here:

kavemanaquatics.com/bacterial-bloom-and-high-ammonia

The following tips will help you eliminate general reasons for cloudiness in your tank but will also prevent a bacterial bloom from occurring. Follow these tips and I'm certain you'll have the crystal clear clarity we all want in our tanks!

Chapter 2

WATER CHANGES

> "Cloudy water is always the effect to a cause.
> Not the other way around."

I know water changes may seem very obvious to some, but I have to cover it in this book. Yes, removing old dirty water and replacing with fresh clean water will help in keeping your water crystal clear but it also IS NOT the fix for your cloudy water problems. Cloudy water is always the effect to a cause. Not the other way around. While water changes are necessary in keeping a clean healthy tank it's not always the answer to your cloudy water problems.

Actually, sometimes water changes can CAUSE the cloudy water issue itself. How? Well, if your source water is high in dissolved organics, and you put that into your tank, you can cause the aforementioned heterotrophic bacteria to grow and multiply. You're feeding them after all. Why wouldn't they grow?

This is why sometimes immediately after a water change you'll have cloudy water for a few hours. You caused a mini bacterial bloom with your organic rich tap water. So keep that in mind.

Ultimately though, yes you do want to water change on a set schedule that works best for your specific tank. No 1 set schedule is universal. Everyone's tank is different. You'll have to determine what's best for your tank setup, with your specific fish species, their quantity, their size, your filtration setup, and many other factors.

I have a great video on exactly how to determine when you should be water changing on the KaveMan Aquatics YouTube Channel.

You can find it by searching YouTube for – "KaveMan When To"

Chapter 3

FILTRATION

"How much filtration is adequate for your tank is determined by many factors. Tank size alone is not the only one."

The last obvious thing I must discuss in this book is your filtration. Obviously without adequate filtration you won't be able to ever have crystal clear water.

If your filtration system isn't circulating enough water per hour through its sponges and media then you'll be leaving to much waste and harmful byproducts in your water column.

Detritus will be visibly floating around in your tank, byproducts like ammonia, nitrite and nitrate will remain in your system not only causing damage or even death to your fish but it will also be a contributing factor to your tanks cloudiness.

How much filtration is adequate for your tank is determined by many factors. Tank size alone is not the only one. How many fish you keep, their size, their species, how much you feed, your maintenance practices all determine what is adequate.

First and foremost, you must ensure you have adequate filtration or none of the following tips will be effective for you.

There, I said it, lol Let's carry on!

Part II

Your contribution to cloudiness

KaveMan Aquatics

Chapter 4

STOP OVER FEEDING

"Over feeding is the number one cause of cloudy water"

No worries, we all do it! Especially as beginners. We feel it's good parenting to feed our fish and give them what they want. Don't they always look hungry? So why not feed them? Well fish are always going to look hungry, even right after a feeding. They'll still want more! But you can't give in.

Fish have very small stomachs and get more than enough from a small feeding. It has been said that on average a fish' stomach is the size of their eyeball, yea that small! As a beginner in the hobby, we just want to keep them full and satisfied, but the thing is, they're never satisfied! lol

Over feeding is the number one cause of cloudy water. Any uneaten food that stays trapped in your tank will decompose and be the source of a cloudy tank. Remember those big pesky heterotrophic bacteria you just read about? Well, when there's extra uneaten food in your tank it sparks the growth of those heterotrophic bacteria. You're basically feeding them with the extra food. And once they get going, they reproduce quickly and like I said, they'll be visible to your naked eye. They are what cause your tank to look cloudy after a feeding.

Making things worse over feeding will add ammonia to your tank, a deadly byproduct of waste. You know what else will add ammonia, all the waste product from your fish over eating. All that food's gotta go somewhere right. They will be pooping in excess and that organic matter is just another thing those pesky heterotrophic bacteria love.

If you haven't figured it out yet our goal is to keep heterotrophic bacteria to a minimum in our tank. They are necessary because waste breakdown is necessary but we want them to stay in our substrate or in our filter and NOT in our water column.

So, key take away about feeding, feed as much as your fish can consume in about 30-60 seconds!

Start with a very, very small portion. Let them eat it all in 5 or 10 seconds. Then dose again for another 5-10 seconds. When it takes them a full 30-60 seconds to eat it all, that's it, they're good! And your tank will stay nice and clear as well 😊

Chapter 5

VACUUM YOUR SUBSTRATE

> "When performing a deep vacuum, I recommend turning your filter (s) off. At this point you don't want the filter to do its job because you're already in cleaning mode."

You may have plenty of water movement in your tank, which is a very good thing, but detritus will still pile up. There will always be a dead spot (s) with little to no circulation and fish waste, uneaten food, other organic matter will find it and stay trapped.

Again, like previously discussed, any dead, non-living organic matter that remains in your tank will cause heterotrophic bacteria to grow and cloud your water.

Vacuuming your substrate will be the only way to remove these "pockets of poop". Depending on your tank setup and specific bio-load will determine how frequently you should vacuum. As a reference, in my 210 Gallon Over Stocked African Cichlid Tank I vacuum my substrate every 2-3 weeks with a deep vacuum every 2-3 months. But keep in mind that in my tank I have excellent water movement preventing dead spots from forming. (More on that later)

If you feel your tank just can't stay clear after a water change or a cleaning you may need to increase your vacuuming schedule. You may also have a combination of an over feeding problem, causing your fish to poop excessively, and not enough water movement preventing dead spots from forming in your tank. Dead spots prevent the detritus from finding your filter intakes which is where all the waste needs to go.

The best way to ensure a clean tank is to occasionally do a deep vacuum and remove as much decor as possible without disrupting too much of your substrate. Remember that your substrate houses a lot of your beneficial bacteria as well as inside your filter. Disrupting too much substrate at once can cause a reduction in beneficial bacteria, which can cause a deadly ammonia spike.

When performing a deep vacuum, I recommend turning your filter (s) off. At this point you don't want the filter to do its job because you're already in cleaning mode. When you remove your décor, you'll free up all the detritus and it'll be floating around in your water column. Don't allow this to go into your filter at this point. It'll just contribute to the overall waste already in there. At this point you're prepped to remove it all from the entire system yourself.

Vacuum around spots where decor can block circulation. These spots will most likely have a big build up of detritus. If you keep gravel substrate, be sure to dig into it and remove debris and detritus from underneath and in between the gravel. I recommend only doing this digging technique on part of your substrate, especially if your tank is still fairly young. For the same reason previously stated, we don't want to kill off beneficial bacteria. Start with ¼ -1/2 of your substrate. Next vacuum continue from where you left off at the previous cleaning.

If you keep sand substrate the best tactic is to just brush the surface of the sand. Sand substrate usually keeps all of the waste and detritus on top of the sand and not under it. But some can and will get under it as well. Occasionally you will want to dig your vacuum tool into the sand as well but you'll have to use a special technique to prevent the sand from being sucked up your vacuum tool.

When you dig under the surface and sand begins to be pulled up your tube, you'll want to stop your syphon. Either by kinking your hose or by closing the valve on your syphon tool. This will temporarily stop the "pull" and suction of water and the sand will fall down the tube and back into your tank. Once all the sand is out of your tube, un-kink the hose or open your valve to resume the suction. I have a full video tutorial on this exact process on the KaveMan Aquatics YouTube Channel.

Visit YouTube.com/KaveManAquatics for full tutorials.

KaveMan Aquatics

Chapter 6

PREVENT ALGAE GROWTH

> "Preventing algae growth as much as possible is key but it will still always try to grow. Staying on top of it will help in keeping it at bay and will also help in keeping your water crystal clear."

E very fish keepers enemy is Algae. And Algae can get out of control very quickly. Not only will it grow on your decor but it will also grow on your glass. Visible green algae will block your viewing areas and give your tank a greenish, dirty look. It will also keep your water looking grungy!

Algae starts to grow in excess for many reasons. One of them is too much light. Light is one of the food sources for algae. By keeping your tank lights on too long, or by allowing too much natural light to hit your tank, algae will grow and reproduce quickly.

I recommend keeping your lights on for a maximum of 8 hours a day. If you've already got an algae problem, 6 hours or less will help in reducing the algae build up.

Another reason is too much nutrients in the form of nitrates and phosphates in your tank. Nitrate production happens in every tank. When it remains in your tank, in excess, due to an inefficient maintenance schedule, algae will grow. All plants, including algae feed off nitrates and phosphates in your tank. When your water change schedule is out of whack, allowing for too many nitrates in your tank, you're leaving a food source for algae. And they will gladly take your food offering!

Preventing algae growth as much as possible is key but it will still always try to grow. Staying on top of it will help in keeping it at bay and will also help in keeping your water crystal clear.

When it begins to grow it will most likely start on your glass. Removing those algae should be obvious but there's also a less visible "film" that sticks to your glass. Less obvious to the naked eye, but it's there. By cleaning your glass with an algae scrubber during every water change you can ensure the removal of this film that will definitely give your water that less-than-optimal look. A few passes with your scrubber along all viewing panels will go a long way in water clarity!

Adding a "cleaning crew" of fish is a sweet hack as well. Plecos, snails, clown loaches and cory cats just to name a few help in "cleaning" your tank.

Adding a Pleco, a Bristle Nose Pleco specifically, which will only grow to about 5-6", can keep your tank algae free. They'll feed off of any algae growth on your décor and/or glass and do most of the heavy lifting for you. I've only got 1 in my 210-gallon tank and he's a work horse!

Maintaining a good maintenance schedule, keeping your lights to a minimum and adding cleaner fish like a Pleco, will help in keeping algae growth to a minimum. Less algae growing in your tank means cleaner and clearer water. But if/when it does grow, keeping it off your glass will also help in the appearance of a cleaner tank.

KEEP YOUR MAINTENANCE CONSISTENT

KAVEMANAQUATICS.COM

Part III

Another level of Clarity

KaveMan Aquatics

Chapter 7

POLY – FIL

> "When this filter gets clogged it is very easy and simple to remove the handful of poly fil in it and replace with a new handful to continue the polishing"

Poly-Fil is the veteran fish keepers secret hack, that's not really a secret anymore. Poly-fil is super fine polyester fibers that can be used to trap the tiniest of particles floating around in your water.

Poly-fil actually polishes your water and you will see an immediate improvement in water clarity. It's used as your final stage of mechanical filtration as all the bigger particles are captured by your course, medium, and fine sponges. Then the poly-fil picks up and traps everything that still made it through.

Adding it is very simple. Grab a handful and separate it from the bag. In a canister filter you want to add the poly-fil in a tray AFTER your mechanical media but BEFORE your bio media. This will make sure that no physical particles reach and clog your bio-media. (Which is another indirect way of keeping your water crystal clear).

In a Hang On Back Filter (HOB) it can be a bit more difficult to use due to the lack of space and specific design of your HOB. If the water in your HOB travels from bottom to top, (like in an Aquaclear or Tidal) again place your poly-fil above your sponge but below your bio-media.

If the water in your HOB travels from back to front (like in a Penguin) then you want your poly fil in front of your sponge but behind your bio-media.

This may be difficult to do depending on the design of your HOB.

While you will need to remove and replace your poly-fil during every filter cleaning, Poly-fil is very cheap and accessible everywhere. One 10 lb bag is about $10 but will last a very long time.

PRO TIP

A great way to use Poly-fil in an HOB is to create a "polishing filter", meaning have an additional HOB with nothing but poly-fil in it. Utilizing all the space in the HOB for nothing but poly-fil will turn it into the ultimate water polishing machine! When this filter gets clogged it is very easy and simple to remove the handful of poly fil in it and replace with a new handful to continue the polishing while your main filter is housing the majority of your beneficial bacteria keeping your tank safe and cycled.

Chapter 8

SPONGE FILTER & AIR PUMP

"Having easily moveable, seeded, sponge filters available is always a good thing."

A sponge filter is a super economical addition to your tank. It doesn't cost much because it doesn't have any moving parts and will never break. With an air pump and an air line attached to it you can achieve multiple benefits, including cleaner and clearer water!

A sponge filter provides additional mechanical filtration to scoop up and trap any particles that just can't find their way to your filter intakes. These loose free-floating particles are what makes your tank look dirty and cloudy. The sponge filter acts as another way to trap them and prevent them from remaining free floating. Because it's an internal filter its efficiency is superb! You will see improvements in your water clarity almost overnight after adding a sponge filter.

It also acts as biological media because the added surface area of the sponge allows beneficial bacteria to grow and thrive on this very oxygenated area. The more surface area we provide for beneficial bacteria to grow on the healthier our tank will be.

Particles of uneaten food may find its way to the sponge filter, this is a great way for fish to find the food and graze right off of the sponge for a snack.

Your sponge filter also helps in aerating your tank by causing surface agitation as the bubbles rise and pop on the surface. This will help in the very important transfer of oxygen in your tank.

Another key benefit is that a sponge filter is easily moveable and interchangeable. Having seeded media that can be easily transferred to another tank is an important veteran hack in the aquarium hobby. When you add a seeded (media having beneficial bacteria) sponge filter to a new tank setup it will be instantly cycled. Meaning you will be able to add fish to that tank immediately without having to wait for the nitrogen cycle to complete in the new tank. This is very helpful when needing to quickly set up a hospital or quarantine tank. Having easily moveable, seeded, sponge filters available is always a good thing.

The only negative I can think off when adding a sponge filter is that it may not look aesthetically pleasing in your tank. It may not fit with your aquascape or décor setup. If you can hide it behind a rock, great. Or you may want to highlight the sponge filter as part of your scape. Too each is own on this one.

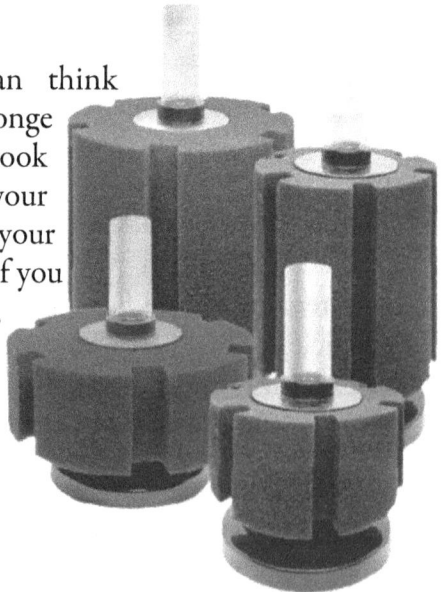

Chapter 9

WAVE MAKER (S)

> "Over and over as your water flows in a circular vortex it will bring detritus along with it exactly where you want it to flow."

Stagnant water in an aquarium is never a good thing. HOB filters can give you surface agitation. Canister filters can push water by way of output hoses. But a wave maker will give you the best circulation around.

Adding a wave maker will help create a vortex of water. As it pushes water away it also sucks water towards it from above and below. If you can set up your wave maker(s) properly to work with your filter output you can maximize water movement and minimize any dead areas where detritus can build up and stay trapped.

As previously discussed, the key to a clean tank is to get as much waste and detritus to your filter as possible so it can do its job. A wave maker is the best way IMO to keep all detritus from remaining trapped somewhere in your tank.

It may seem counterintuitive but your wave maker will make all the debris and waste free floating in your water column.

"But Kev, I thought we didn't want particles floating around in our water?"

Correct we don't, but the way to get it out is by way of your filter intake. Detritus will never find your filter if it's stuck in a dead spot behind a rock. Detritus does more harm when its unknowingly stuck under a piece of décor or behind a plant than it does free floating in the water column. We must get it to keep moving in order to eventually make its way to the filter intake where it will be removed from your water column and trapped in your filter to decompose there instead of in your tank. A wave maker will help with that!

Proper Placement of your wave maker is important too. Placing it on top, angled upwards and on the same side of your filter intake is key.

By placing it on top and angled upwards you create surface agitation which helps in oxygen transfer in your tank. This is very important for all tanks.

By placing it on same side of your filter intake, (which will be closer to the bottom of your tank) water returning to your wave maker from underneath will also pull detritus with it. Causing that detritus to float right past your intake. Genius, right? This helps in getting the maximum amount of trapped detritus to your intake in the most efficient way. Over and over as your water flows in a circular vortex it will bring detritus along with it exactly where you want it to flow.

If you keep aggressive fish like African Cichlids a wave maker can also help in reducing some aggression. The extra flow and current in the tank keep them actively swimming to distract from focusing on a specific fish they may not be too friendly with. A wave maker is a common tool used in African Cichlid tanks.

BTW... If you've never heard of African Cichlids or are curious to learn more about the fish I keep, I have an entire online video course dedicated to teaching you everything you need to know to start your tank, raise your fish and keep them happy and thriving in a successful tank! Watch the entire course from your computer, tablet, or cell phone!

More information can be found here –

KaveManAquatics.com/African-Cichlids-Course

P.S. Keep an eye out for the new paper back book version of the entire course! 😊

With that being said wave makers should only be used with fish that enjoy a good current. Some fish like Discuss, Angel Fish and Gold Fish prefer still, calm waters where a wave maker may cause them stress. Consider your species before implementing the use of a wave maker.

Additionally, I suggest a minimum of a 30 Gallon tank for wave maker use. A wave maker of any size will be too strong for a tank any smaller than that.

Go to YouTube.com/KaveManAquatics for full tutorials on best and proper wave maker placement. Search for "KaveMan Wave Maker"

KAVEMAN AQUATICS

Chapter 10

CHEMICAL MEDIA

> "When they cannot absorb any more, they can release all the trapped organics back in to your water."

If you've tried all the above and you still can't get to that clarity level you'd like then chemical media will definitely give you that boost to put you over the top!

While chemical filtration is not necessary for proper filtration it can be beneficial when trying to get to the next level of clarity.

Chemical media can remove dissolved particles in your water that give your water a hazy look. Activated Carbon will absorbs any medications you may have used in your tank and will also remove unpleasant odors from your tank.

Two of the best in the industry are Chemi-Pure Blue and Purigen.

Both work as advertised and will make a noticeable difference in water clarity.

Chemical media does need to be replaced about every month or so depending on your specific bio-load. When they cannot absorb any more, they can release all the trapped organics back in to your water. So be mindful of when they need replacement.

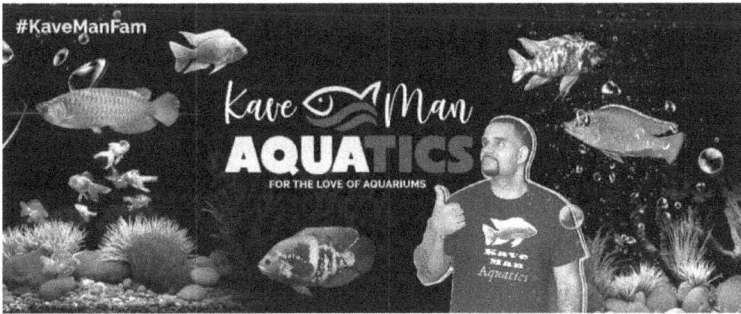

Everyone wants crystal clear water in their aquarium and guess what, it's really not that hard to achieve. By implementing these simple steps your waters clarity will definitely improve. But we also have to think about our regular scheduled routine maintenance. That is the foundation of a beautiful looking tank. Without it, no matter what you try, change, or do won't help. So don't get comfortable and slack off on your cleanings and water changes.

Once you do achieve that beautiful looking crystal clear water I have to reiterate one more time. This clear and clean looking water does not mean the water is optimal for your fish. It can be very deceiving.

Having ammonia, nitrite or nitrate in your tank can cause harm or even death, and they can be in a tank with crystal clear water!

So make sure you test your water for harmful byproducts just as much as you scrub that glass! Happy Fish Keeping ☺

KAVEMAN AQUATICS FAMILY

Hopefully you found the information in this book helpful and are planning to take action to get your water looking amazing!

Another great resource for information and guidance on the aquarium hobby is my Free Facebook group - KaveMan Aquatics Family. In the group you can find help, share experiences and connect with like-minded fish keepers. It's an awesome resource for all aquarium hobbyist.

Consider joining the free group here:
FaceBook.com/Groups/KaveManAquatics

BONUS LINKS

KaveMan Master Link - Updated information on anything/
everything KaveMan related

(koji.to/KaveMan_Aquatics)

KaveMan Affilate Shop - All Recommended Products and
Equipment

(KaveManAquatics.com/Shop)

KaveMan Merch - Branded Hoodies and Tee's

(KaveManAquatics.com/KaveMan-Merch)

KaveMan Academy - Online Courses and Coaching

(KaveManAquatics.com/KaveMan-Aquatics-Academy)

FOR THE LOVE OF AQUARIUMS

www.ingramcontent.com/pod-product-compliance
Lightning Source LLC
Chambersburg PA
CBHW072157020426
42334CB00018B/2047